Jean Banyolak with I
Better Is Your Lov

**Library
Oakland S.U.M.**

Library
Oakland S.U.M.

JEAN BANYOLAK
with
INGRID TROBISCH

Better Is Your Love Than Wine

INTER-VARSITY PRESS
Downers Grove, Illinois 60515

Other books by the Trobisches:
I Loved a Girl
I Married You
The Joy of Being a Woman
Living with Unfulfilled Desires
Love Is a Feeling to Be Learned
Love Yourself
My Beautiful Feeling
On Our Way Rejoicing

Booklets by Walter Trobisch:
Martin Luther's Quiet Time
Spiritual Dryness

© 1971 by Editions Trobisch,
D-737 Baden-Baden (Germany).
All rights for translation, reproduction
and adaptation reserved for all countries.

Seventh American printing, December 1979,
by permission from Editions Trobisch.

InterVarsity Press is the book-publishing
division of Inter-Varsity Christian Fellowship,
a student movement active on campus at
hundreds of universities, colleges and schools
of nursing. For information about local and
regional activities, write IVCF, 233 Langdon St.,
Madison, WI 53703.

Better Is Your Love Than Wine, originally
published as *Ma femme n'aime plus nos relations
sexuelles* by Jean Banyolak, is translated and
adapted by Ingrid Trobisch.

ISBN 0-87784-435-6

Printed in the United States of America

INTRODUCTION

This book, written by an African for his fellow Africans, was originally published under the title *My Wife Has Lost Interest in Sex*. The author would be the first one to agree that there are more detailed books on this subject, but the request to publish this manuscript in the United States came to us from American readers who found that its simplicity, straightforwardness and brevity was especially appealing to them. However, an explanation about the author, his background and purpose in writing this booklet is certainly appropriate.

Jean Banyolak is our colleague in family-life work in Africa. My wife and I greatly respect him for his instinctive wisdom, humility and patience.

He was born in a small village in the virgin forest of Cameroun, West Africa, in 1942. His education was received at church-sponsored schools which had a definitely pietistic emphasis. After his graduation from Cameroun Christian College, he served as a teacher in Cameroun and then received training in marriage counseling in Europe. He and his vivacious wife Ernestine are the parents of a daughter, Elisabeth, and live at present in Douala, Cameroun (Postal Address: B. P. 54 Deido, Douala, Cameroun).

Two main factors determined the author's attitudes toward sexual matters from early childhood: one was the traditional African thinking; the other, a rather narrow religious upbringing. Both had this in common — sex is taboo, something which one does not talk about.

After having been exposed to sex education in a wider Christian context in Europe, Jean felt the necessity to interpret to his countrymen what he had learned. This was his motive in writing this book. While doing so, he was constantly fighting a two-front battle: on the one side against an African traditionalism for which talk about sex is close to sacrilege and on the other an unbiblical Christian conservatism for which sex is almost an equivalent to sin or at least something indecent which has nothing to do with the spiritual realm of life.

Jean stands up against both false concepts. He gives his fellow Africans, brought up in his traditions, the vocabulary which enables them to talk about sexual problems, while at the same time declaring that sex and God belong together. Therefore in the African setting, his book is a pioneer achievement. As such it is widely disputed in Africa. While the younger generation hails it with enthusiasm, the older generation condemns it as pornography.

In many African societies, especially also among Moslems, sexual pleasure is considered as a male privilege only. To declare that a woman too is entitled to sexual enjoyment and fulfillment is, as far as Africa is concerned, revolutionary in itself. With this background in mind one can measure the courage of the author.

The letters which Jean received from his fellow Africans speak for themselves. They give testimony of the great helplessness and ignorance, especially on the part of husbands, for they show how little a husband understands his wife's feelings. But they also indicate that sexual anticipation among African women is growing.

Those who read these letters attentively will soon realize that the problems they contain are certainly not limited to Africa. In spite of all the sex-saturated books, films and magazines, ignorance about basic sexual facts is still widespread even in Western cultures. The problem of non-understanding between the sexes is a universal one. Also the problem of unfulfilled sexual expectations.

Therefore I hope that this book, even though the author never dreamed of its publication outside of Africa, may be of help wherever it is read.

Walter Trobisch

AFRICANS WRITE ABOUT THEIR SEXUAL PROBLEMS

ABEL: "My wife has lost interest in sex. We were married two years ago.

"In the beginning, everything was fine. At times my wife even invited me. I saw and felt that she was really happy. She never resisted my approaches. Sometimes she even hurried to lock the door so that we could be alone. Both of us felt completely satisfied after the act.

"But now everything has changed. She doesn't invite me any more. If I do it, then her joy becomes sorrow. Sometimes she even gets nervous. She always sends me to lock the door and then she only gets half undressed. During the act, she makes faces. What shall I do?"

BENJAMIN: "Here's my problem. My wife has become cold. What are the cures for frigidity?"

COLBERT: "My wife no longer arrives at an orgasm with me. I am 38 years old and she is 24. I am told that she runs after young men of her own age. This troubles me a lot. Wouldn't it be wise for me to marry another woman?"

DANIEL: "My dear wife has started to lie to me. When I want to sleep with her, she sometimes tells me that she has her period or that she has a stomach ache or a headache or her back hurts. . . . When I bring her to the hospital for a check-up, each time the doctor says that she's in good health. When she goes to the market to buy food or the well to fetch water early in the morning, she sometimes deceives me. This is the moment when she goes to other men — her friends. The disturbance of our sexual harmony began three months ago. What can I do?"

EDWARD: "Should one talk or be silent during the sex act? I had an argument with my wife about this last night. My colleagues are not sure what to answer. Every one of us has a different opinion."

FREDERICK: "My spouse prefers to have the light out during the act. Is this normal?"

WILLIAM: "As a close friend of yours, I am happy that you are now in Europe. How do they practice sex over there?"

ANNE: "I have a problem in my heart. I'm afraid to tell it to my husband, because I don't dare to criticize him. I find him rather brutal when we love each other in the evening. How shall I tell him this?"

BERTHA: "I just read the book called *I Loved a Girl*. I understand now that my husband ejaculates too early. How can this be treated? Can I help him to hold back?"

CHRISTINE: "My husband runs after college girls.

He tells me that they learn how to make love at school. I answered him that I also shall learn how to make love from the college boys in order to satisfy him as the college girls. He got very angry and would have beaten me if I had not run away. I wait for your advice about this."

ESTHER: "My husband demands that I yield to him every night. This is unbearable for me. When I tell him that this is too much he talks about marrying another woman. Tell me, how often is it normal for married couples to unite?"

FRANCES: "My husband never tells me beforehand when he wants to have intercourse. Sometimes when I want to prepare the food he calls me in the bedroom and undresses me. I'm afraid to criticize him, but this displeases me very much. Should a wife say No to her husband in this moment?"

GERTRUDE: "My husband goes to sleep very quickly after the sex act while I stay awake. He turns his back toward me and snores. This causes my satisfaction and joy to go away."

MARIE: "My husband is really the first man to whom I gave myself. But when we had intercourse for the first time we couldn't see any blood on the sheet. My husband reproaches me all the time that I wasn't a virgin, because he found my hymen already ruptured. What can I tell him to prove to him that I really was a virgin?"

AN OPENING WORD

It is certainly not easy to talk about sex. This is probably because it is customary not to. Many try to hide the fact that they have problems in this field and struggle along secretly. Nevertheless, these problems are burning ones for many couples and it is a pity that they are not able to express them. There are even educated adults who do not know the names of certain sex organs. Most of the parents of my country never talk about sex relations to their children. As far as they are concerned, this is a realm which is completely taboo.

The confidential letters which you have just read ask difficult questions and call for frank answers. Of course, in such a small book I cannot give complete answers, but I will be frank and mention briefly the way in which help can be found. These letters impel me not to be quiet on this subject which is so mysterious for many people. St. Clement of Alexandria has said, "It is not right that we are ashamed to call things by their names which God was not ashamed to create." And besides, the Bible speaks openly about sexual union in marriage.

I would like to emphasize a very important fact: According to the Bible, physical union is an integral part of marriage. Genesis 2 : 24 says, "Therefore a man leaves his father and his mother and cleaves to his wife, and they become one flesh." This means that sexual relations before or outside of marriage do not correspond with the will of God. The reason this is not the will of God has been explained in detail by Walter Trobisch in *I Loved a Girl* and *My Wife Made Me a Polygamist.*

Therefore, this present book is written *exclusively for married couples.* All the letters which I have quoted are written by married men or women and my answers therefore concern only married couples.

THE BIBLE SPEAKS ABOUT SEXUAL LIFE

From the very beginning, God has given the gift of sexuality to man. Reproduction was one of the tasks God gave to the first couple in paradise. "So God created man in his own image, in the image of God he created him; male and female he created them. And God blessed them, and God said to them, Be fruitful and multiply, and fill the earth and subdue it" (Gen. 1 : 27-28 a).

In Genesis 4 we read about the sex union of the first human couple. "Now Adam knew Eve his wife, and she conceived and bore Cain" (Gen. 4 : 1).

In the middle of the Bible we find the Song of Solomon which is, in my opinion, the most beautiful of all love poems. Let me quote from the first chapter·

O that you would kiss me with the kisses of your mouth!
For your love is better than wine,
your anointing oils are fragrant,
your name is oil poured out;
therefore the maidens love you.
                    (Song 1 : 2-3)

15

In the next chapter we find the description of a loving couple:

Refresh me with apples; for I am sick with love.
O that his left hand were under my head,
and that his right hand embraced me!
(Song 2 : 5-6)

The beauty and charm of a fiancee are described as more precious than all other earthly goods:

How sweet is your love, my sister, my bride!
how much better is your love than wine,
and the fragrance of your oils than any spice!
Your lips distil nectar, my bride;
honey and milk are under your tongue.
(Song 4 : 10-11)

The Bible does not despise the physical beauty of the human being:

How graceful are your feet in sandals,
O queenly maiden!
Your rounded thighs are like jewels,
the work of a master hand.
Your two breasts are like two fawns,
twins of a gazelle.
Your neck is like an ivory tower.
Your eyes are pools in Heshbon,
by the gate of Bathrabbim.
Your nose is like a tower of Lebanon,
overlooking Damascus.
(Song 7 : 1, 3-4)

A true lover wishes to have a secure place in the heart of the one whom he loves:

Set me as a seal upon your heart,
as a seal upon your arm;
for love is strong as death,
jealousy as cruel as the grave.
Its flashes are flashes of fire,
a most vehement flame.

(Song 8 : 6)

The New Testament is not hostile to the human body either. Jesus himself was no enemy of the body. In the incarnation of God in Christ and through the resurrection of the body which we confess in our Creed, the human body is sanctified.

According to the New Testament, our bodies are a temple of God. "Do you not know that you are God's temple and that God's Spirit dwells in you?" (1 Cor. 3 : 16) The Bible does not despise the human body. Every Christian should be thankful to God for his body. A couple united in love should receive the pleasures sensed through their bodies as a precious gift from God. I appreciate very much the following statement from the book *Amour et fiançailles*[1].

"Sexuality is not the fruit of sin as some people claim. Before the fall of man, God had already created in him his sexual life. But this sexual life has been put out of balance by sin. Instead of

1 Editions Labor et Fides, Geneva.

leading man to fellowship and joy it has often contributed to his destruction. If God has created sexuality and if Jesus has never declared that it is impure, there is absolutely no reason why it should cause in us feelings of shame." Why not talk about it then?

SEXUAL UNION IN MARRIAGE

Sex relations are not only physical or anatomical but also psychological in nature. In other words, what is essential is connected much more with the thoughts and feelings toward one's self and one's partner than with the sex organs. The act of love is an intimate encounter of the whole masculine person with the whole feminine person. It is the total union of body, soul and spirit. With these facts in mind, I answered the first letter quoted in this book, that of Abel who wrote: "My wife has lost interest in sex."

In the realm of love, there are no general rules applicable to everyone. Each couple has to find its own way. Nevertheless, certain elementary steps of the sex act are the same all over. This was a part of my answer to William who asked: "How do they practice sex in Europe?"

The act of love consists of three different stages: preparation for intercourse or love play, the sex act and the period of relaxation.

PREPARATION FOR INTERCOURSE OR LOVE PLAY

The period of preparation varies in length depending upon whether a couple feels the desire to unite as is their habit or whether they come together after a period of abstinence. There is also the possibility of a loving surprise. It can happen that the sexual desire springs up suddenly in one of the partners, that he transfers it to the other one and that both of them end up by wishing to unite immediately. In the case of such a loving surprise, the preparation can be shortened considerably.

Normally, however, the preparation should be much longer. If a couple plans to unite in the evening, their preparation could begin as early as in the morning. This long-range preparation is important for both the husband and the wife — although especially for the wife. Dr. Theodor Bovet, a well-known marriage counselor in Europe, author of *A Handbook to Marriage*, speaks of the love of the husband for his wife as being like a warm coat in which she is enclosed and sheltered. When she feels secure in this love at all times she can give herself to him and fully respond in the act of love. But if the husband is unkind or insensitive to his wife in the morning, then it is as if the coat is full of holes, and he must not be astonished if in the evening she is not ready to respond to his approaches when he wants to unite with her.

Likewise the wife must try to understand and be sensitive to her husband. The male ego is fragile. If the wife understands this, then she will not scold, mock or condemn her husband in any area of life, especially in things pertaining to sexual love. Instead she will be appreciative of his care for her.

To prepare for the act of love both the husband and wife must know what the partner needs and desires. If either is full of fear, unresolved conflict or feelings of hurt or inadequacy, then he or she will draw back and not find the joy which is rightfully theirs in the act of love. The secret then is to be able to talk to each other and to share that which hurts. To keep silent is harmful to both. In answering Frances's letter, I encouraged her to tell her husband frankly, with love and without being afraid, what she thinks about their sexual union. Of course, she should not do it at an inconvenient moment

The question which Abel poses is different. He complains that his wife no longer invites him to have intercourse. Contrary to what most women think, it is not always the task of the husband to initiate physical union. The tender request of the wife may augment the desire of the husband and make him very grateful to her. If the partner does not voluntarily accept this loving invitation, it is preferable to wait rather than try to convince him or her to consent immediately.

The act of love is impossible without voluntary agreement. The location of the vagina proves that. It is not located behind as with some animals. It is between the legs of the woman, and the legs are the strongest parts of the human body. Any penetration, therefore, is impossible unless she opens her thighs voluntarily. If the sexual union with one's partner is to be successful, it is important to know beforehand that she fully agrees. If this is not the case, then the husband must continue to court her until she is willing to yield. Instead of doubling the power to force the other one to receive him, it is much better to double the courtesies, until the other one consents of his own will. In a gallant manner, the one who has the desire invites the other one. Then the two will agree about the proper time and place. Finally, they will give each other a kiss of expectation and promise.

From then on the partners try to create an atmosphere of love. Each one aims at being well-received in the other one's soul. They can succeed in this by doing as many things as possible together — going for a walk, listening to music, dancing as a couple, helping one another and exchanging views and comments. The lovers seek to express their sentiment in tender words. They play together, work together, even read together something of common interest. Often being out in the open, breathing fresh air, will invigorate and animate them. Some couples like to surprise each other with gifts or small tokens of their love. In any case, it is essential that a feeling of joy be awakened in the partner.

The role that physical cleanliness plays during the act should not be neglected. Christine complains in her letter: "My husband runs after college girls." I suggested to her that perhaps one of the reasons her husband is attracted to college girls is because they are always clean. College girls have learned about hygiene in school.

Some couples make it a habit to take a bath as a preparation for their sex union. A bad odor can extinguish erotic feelings, just as the smell of a certain perfume can awaken them. Therefore it is well to conform to our partner's tastes. One must also be careful about bad breath. Some women cannot stand the smell of onions, alcoholic drinks, tobacco or anything that is spoiled. Are we also ready inwardly to receive our partner and to give ourselves to him completely?

The place where the lovers unite should give them a feeling of security. Both of them, but especially the wife, can be very much disturbed by walls which are too thin, by doors which cannot be locked, by beds which are too narrow, too short or too noisy, by rooms too hot or too cold. It goes without saying that children should not sleep in the bedroom of their parents, or else this will be a cause of disturbance, especially for the wife.

The moment approaches. Is everything ready and care taken that no kill-joy knocks at the door? Nothing should bother or trouble this great moment of pleasure. The love play is now ready to begin.

A man desires to take and possess his wife, while her greatest desire is to surrender and be possessed. Here everything depends upon the skill of the husband. It is up to him to master the delicate art of winning over the heart of his companion; to prepare her by making her erotic desire grow and blossom. The main task of the wife in this moment is simply to relax and to be pleased by being pleased.

The most common mistake is for this time of preparation to be too short. This is probably the case with Benjamin whose wife has become frigid. Half an hour of preparation is the absolute minimum. The longer it takes, the more grateful will be the wife. Even a whole hour would not be too much or too long for her. Generally, one can say that the time of preparation can never be too long. It can only be too short.

Here, I would like to repeat again that there are no rules or prescriptions which apply to every couple. The sexual union is a response born out of tender feelings and sensitive reflexes which should be completely spontaneous.

As to the question of undressing, Abel seems to be perturbed that his wife does not get completely undressed. Certain wives enjoy very much being undressed by their husbands. In this case, the husband does it gently and calmly, piece by piece. According to the lovers' tastes, the wife can be undressed completely or partially. Some couples prefer that the wife wear a very thin negligee or a soft, velvety nightgown.

As far as the man is concerned, he can undress himself or be undressed by his wife if she enjoys doing it. Some wives like their husbands completely naked; others prefer that the husband keep on his shorts until the moment of full union. It all depends upon the taste of the wife.

It is very important that after undressing the couple not be interrupted until after the period of relaxation. Otherwise it is psychologically very troublesome.

Before the complete coming-together, the two exchange mutual gestures of tenderness which lead them gradually to a high sexual tension. This tension should then be satisfied and quieted by the union of love.

In order to carry one's partner to the height of sexual excitement, one has to know the erotic zones, the parts of the human body most sensitive to erotic feeling. "To know" one's wife or one's husband means to know where these zones are.

If one is in good health, practically the whole human body reacts to erotic stimulation as a result of practice and certain psychological factors. Generally speaking, these erotic zones are located in the vicinity of the sex organs and around the orifices by which the interior of our organism communicates with the outside world. These are the lips, the mouth with all its parts including the tongue, the ear lobe and the pavilion behind the ear. In addition, the armpits, the inside of the thighs and the area around the sex organs are also erotically sensitive.

The erotic zones for the woman are especially the nipples and the area surrounding them on the breasts, the clitoris, the large and small lips which protect the vaginal opening as well as the muscles at the interior of the vagina.

Some African tribes practice circumcision for the female as well as the male. By this operation the clitoris of the woman is cut out or severely damaged. One of the motives for this operation, called clitoridectomy, is to prevent the woman from having an orgasm or even any sexual pleasure. My talks with African, American and European doctors lead me to discourage this operation. Sexual enjoyment in orgasm is God's gift to both husband and wife. God has promised to give his children "richly all things to enjoy" (1 Tim. 6 : 17). Through love, patience and practice it is possible also for the wife to know this joy.

The married couple embraces, exchanging caresses and kisses. All these gestures have but one goal — to excite the lovers sufficiently so that they are able to unite completely and easily.

What is the final stage of sexual excitement? The end of the male organ itself is completely rigid. The breasts of the wife swell and the nipples are erect. Her clitoris, at the upper end of the vaginal region, increases in size. Due to the increased blood supply in the vaginal region, a result of the gentle love play of her husband, the vagina becomes warmer and more moist, making it ready to receive the penis. The wife's breathing becomes more rapid and it is her ardent desire that the act may begin. In case the husband feels that his ejaculation is very close, then the couple should wait for a few moments before the second stage of the conjugal act begins.

THE SEX ACT PROPER

This is the decisive phase, the act of love itself. For its beginning, one condition must be fulfilled: The vagina must be moist. As explained above, this takes place when sensations from the clitoris cause little glands in the vagina to send out a fluid which lubricates the vagina and thus makes the entrance of the penis easier. If this has not taken place, sexual union will be painful for the wife and perhaps even displeasing for the man. Without this lubrication in the vagina there is even a possibility that small wounds may result.

If you recall the letters quoted at the beginning of this book, I believe that Benjamin, Daniel and the husbands of Anne and Frances should ask themselves whether an inadequate preparation is one of the causes of their problems.

The couple may use any position they wish. The most common position is the one where the wife is lying on her back with her legs spread apart and a little bent. The husband is above her and supports himself by his elbows and knees in order not to bother her by his weight.

A position in which the woman is above is also possible. Each couple should use the position which brings them the most joy and satisfaction. In fact, it is often advisable to change positions.

The penis can be guided in the beginning by the husband, but later more safely by the wife. It must be remembered that the vaginal conduct runs first up and then backward, and it is in this direction that the man tries to enter. A small membrane called the hymen partially closes the entrance of a virgin. Carefully the husband breaks it and often, with this penetration, causes his young wife some pain and a little bleeding. In case the hymen persists after several attempts to break it (a rare condition), it is advisable to consult a medical doctor who will cut it easily.

I now come to the letter written by Marie, who says that her husband reproaches her that she was not a virgin because he found her hymen already ruptured. It is not just the existence of the hymen which characterizes the virginity of a woman. Often the hymen is ruptured by itself by a sudden movement of the legs, by the use of tampons during menstruation, or even by age. Virginity is above all the untouched reservoir of the ability to love.

After uniting, the lovers move together rhythmically and slowly. The husband may prefer to use up and down movements where the penis glides back and forth within the vagina, or round movements which go more from right to left, while the wife responds by movements of her own. Sometimes the wife has the most joy when she rotates in the opposite direction to that of her husband.

The partners try to prolong these pleasant movements together as long as they are capable. It is desirable to make them last as long as possible, because the feeling of pleasure which the wife experiences rises more slowly than that of her husband. But aside from this fact, it is also true that this mutual exchange of happiness has a great meaning in itself for the fulfillment of marriage.

Every rough movement is to be discouraged. Anne mentions in her letter that her husband is brutal. This can only lead to hurt feelings; it is destructive for any marriage.

Bertha states in her letter that her husband ejaculates too soon. In this case I would give him the following advice. He should ask his wife not to caress his penis any more after it has reached the state of erection. He may even try, slowly and gently, to enter her vagina before his organ has reached the complete stage of erection, for the entrance itself is a strong means of excitement. Immediately after entrance, the couple may pause for a short time so that the first wave of excitement will pass. It is also advisable that the man should not enter too deeply in the vaginal conduct, for the deeper he enters, the more contact he has and the more intense is the stimulation. Also the wife experiences her greatest sexual stimulation at a point only about $2^1/_2$ inches inside the vagina. Therefore it is important that the husband avoid too strong and too fast movements back and forth which only mask the sensations of his wife as well as cause him to have his ejaculation too soon. He should move very slowly with gentle pressure sideways toward the walls of the vagina. Filling the lungs with a deep breath and tightening the abdominal muscles has also proved helpful.

Psychologically it is sometimes helpful for the man to imagine that he is in the process of sucking something out rather than pouring something into. He should also try to concentrate his thoughts on non-erotic objects.

How should the wife behave in such a case? In answer to this question, one wife has given this confidential advice: "While my husband refrains his erotic feeling in order not to ejaculate too soon, I try to intensify my feelings. I am thankful to my husband that he makes an effort on my behalf in order that I also may reach the orgasm. This kindness and love on his part, this desire to help me, makes me very happy. By not just resting quietly, but by tenderly responding to his movements, I consciously yield to him my whole heart, my whole body and all that I am as a feminine being. In this precious moment, I try to do only one thing: to relax and to let myself go completely. The more I get used to my husband, the more I am able to anticipate how close or how far away he is from ejaculation. If I am already highly stimulated and know that my orgasm is very close, while his is farther away,

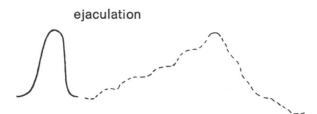

ejaculation

a) male orgasm

b) female orgasm

c) male orgasm only

d) simultaneous orgasm

e) female orgasm before male orgasm

then I stimulate him by his favorite caresses in order that he may let himself go. But if I feel that he is already very close to the climax while I am further away from it, I try to concentrate my whole thinking on erotic sentiments."

This is the procedure by which you can try to experience the climax of sexual pleasure with your partner. It is this information which I shared with Colbert in answer to his letter.

By more vigorous movements, the husband leads his wife to experience an orgasm and ejaculates his sperm within the vagina. This seminal emission marks the masculine orgasm (a). The feminine orgasm is more difficult to determine (b). It can be recognized by the trembling of the wife's whole body as well as by rhythmical contractions of the vagina and uterus combined with a sucking-in motion, but above all by an insurmountable feeling of happiness and well-being, sometimes even by a temporary loss of consciousness.

To harmonize the sexual union means to endeavor to reach the orgasm at the same time as one's partner, as we see in figure (d). Some husbands who reach the orgasm before their wife does, continue nevertheless with their movements and with caressing the erotic zones until she also arrives at an orgasm. Other husbands disengage their penis and by gently touching the clitoris of the wife help her in this way to have an orgasm. However, this latter experience is not as satisfactory for both partners as the above-described one.

To harmonize the conjugal act is a desired goal, but marital happiness does not depend upon its achievement. There are many happily married couples who have never achieved it. And certainly it is not something that can be reached in a day.

Therefore couples should not be discouraged if they have not found complete fulfillment in the act of love during the first months or even the first years of their marriage. Marriage is not a destination, but a journey. As a husband and wife make this journey together, growing and maturing and learning how to love, they will reach sexual harmony as a fruit of their good marriage.

The problem which Benjamin writes about in his letter leads me to say a few words about frigidity. Dr. Bovet also discusses the problem of frigidity in his handbook. A woman is called frigid when she is incapable of experiencing sexual pleasure. Sometimes a woman is only partially frigid, as for example, when she has sexual desire but the sexual union is repugnant to her, or when she is able to have sexual pleasure during the sex act but is incapable of reaching an orgasm or the relaxation which follows. In extreme cases of frigidity, the vagina is drawn together so that any penetration becomes impossible. This is called vaginismus.

The causes of frigidity are now quite well known. Only seldom is frigidity due to a physical deficiency, such as glandular troubles, general exhaustion or insufficient development of the organs. More often frigidity is psychological. In such cases it is often caused by a narrow and negative sex education, which pictures sexuality as something forbidden or indecent and in turn leads to a strong inhibition in the unconscious mind of the girl. Guilt feelings which go back to childhood and which may be caused by sex fantasies or masturbation can also be the cause of frigidity. Even a too close attachment to a girl's father, brothers, teacher or former sweetheart can cause frigidity. Sometimes it is caused by a tendency to homosexuality or simply the fear of everything masculine and the refusal to accept the feminine role.

The danger of becoming frigid is naturally much greater for a woman who has undergone female circumcision. Frigidity is even the motive for this cruel operation because one defends it by saying: "Circumcised women are more faithful." And the reason given is that they are thus deprived of sexual pleasure. Nevertheless, although clitoridectomized women may not be able to have a clitoral orgasm, they can reach a vaginal orgasm. Learning how to do a very simple exercise can be of great help to these women. (Some doctors estimate that two-thirds of all women need help here and yet very few wives have ever heard of this training.)

Dr. Paul Popenoe of the American Institute of Family Relations reports that in a series of over a thousand cases of sexually unsatisfied women who asked for help, some 65 percent gained relief simply by doing this exercise. (Among the other 35 percent were those who had deep-rooted emotional problems as well as some cases of serious physical disease.)

Approximately 1¹/₂ to 2 inches inside the entrance of the vagina is a band of muscle known as the pubococcygeus or Kegel muscle (because of the research of Dr. Arnold Kegel of Los Angeles). The greatest source of sexual sensation has been found to be just beyond the upper edge of this muscle. This is particularly felt when the muscle is contracted or otherwise stimulated. Many women lack full sexual response because this upper portion of the muscle is not well-developed.

Dr. Popenoe gives the following suggestions for training this muscle: "The Kegel muscle can be strengthened by 'pulling up' on it as if making a strong effort to shut off or hold back the flow of urine. A wife who lacks satisfactory sensation in the vagina or who is unable to have orgasm, should practice this regularly, keeping her feet spread a little apart. She may do so for a few minutes at a time, half a dozen times a day, even when she is engaged in some of her housework. Or she may count the contractions and plan on, say 300 a day, divided into groups of 50 each. Strengthening the muscles in this way usually narrows and lengthens the vagina and pulls the organs of the pelvis up into their proper position."

"It is a rare woman," says Dr. Popenoe, "who cannot heighten her sexual adequacy through this understanding and technique, by bringing these muscles surrounding the vagina into play during intercourse. We believe that this is a key to good sexual adjustment."

Sometimes the frigidity of a wife can be caused or aggravated by mistakes of the husband. Repeated awkwardness during the sex act, premature ejaculation, forcing the wife to yield instead of asking her to consent voluntarily, considering her as an object to satisfy his own desire, bad choice of time and place for the sexual union so that the wife feels insecure — all these mistakes on the part of the husband can lead his wife to frigidity.

Premarital sex is often practiced in situations which do not offer any security to the lovers, and these relations are usually accompanied by the fear of conception. Therefore these practices before marriage can actually be one of the causes of frigidity later on in marriage.

I explained these facts about frigidity when answering the letters of Abel, whose wife has lost interest in sex; of Benjamin, whose wife is probably frigid; and of Daniel, whose wife complains about backaches when the moment of sexual union approaches. In the case of frigidity, the couple tries to find out the causes or still better seeks the advice of a marriage counselor or medical doctor who can study the case and offer effective help.

In his letter, Frederick wants to know whether it is normal to turn off all the lights during the sex act. This depends upon the couple. Some women cannot arrive at an orgasm unless the sexual union takes place in complete obscurity. For this reason, they always close their eyes during the act. These wives prefer the night when all the lights are out. Other couples prefer a very dim light and still others red or blue.

Edward asks in his letter: "Should one speak or keep silent during the sex act?" Again there are no fixed rules. However, I would advise the couple to talk. God has given to human beings the gift of speech which animals do not have. It pays to ask our partner how he feels — to tell him what we would like for him to do and how we feel about it.

It is certainly permitted and even recommended to make complaints and suggestions known to one's partner. This is what I advised Anne to do — to tell her husband frankly if she feels that he is brutal to her. Of course, one must choose the right moment. One should not talk about that which hurts on the spur of the moment, but choose a quiet time when there is enough time to listen to each other patiently. The one who is not able to listen to his partner's criticism does not really love him.

We now come to the last stage of the sexual union.

THE PERIOD OF RELAXATION

Following orgasm, the husband will have a feeling of satiation and even exhaustion. He desires sleep for he has used up his physical strength. Just as it takes the wife longer to reach the sexual climax and just as she approaches it in a more gradual manner, so it is with her after orgasm. It is as if she has reached the top of the mountain, and on the summit she has found a plateau, a tableland. She likes to stay there as long as possible and is reluctant to descend. Her great need at this time is to be held by her husband, to feel his support and strength and to be reassured through words and caresses of his love for her. If he withdraws from her embrace, turns his back to her and falls asleep immediately, maybe even snoring, then the marvel — the wonder of this moment — is broken. It is as if a light goes out and the wife has a feeling of emptiness and quiet disappointment. She may even feel abandoned. Consequently a hostile feeling may arise in her. Her husband may appear to her as a thief who comes to steal her body and heart and who then runs off. But she must also understand her husband's tiredness.

After the orgasm, the partners feel moved to the depths of their being. Often they feel exhausted and sigh deeply. In his *Handbook to Marriage* Dr. Bovet has described the feeling between husband and wife at this moment: "After the storm of passion the two lovers are intimately opened up to each other, and can look straight into each other's souls. . . . They can now say and reveal to each other things which would not otherwise find expression, problems are solved without saying a word, and they now experience what full communion can mean." I have counseled the husband of Gertrude to make use of this moment of unity to talk intimately to his wife.

After the orgasm, the partners continue to caress, to admire, to kiss each other and to express their mutual thanks before they separate their bodies from one another. They are especially thankful to God who is the creator of their partner and of the joy which they have just experienced.

Often younger couples again feel excited after a while and wish to repeat the sex act. The partners then continue their love play or even sleep a little, resting in each other's arms. When they unite again, it is easier for the husband to prolong the act of love and then too the wife will usually reach her orgasm more quickly than before.

In marriage one may unite as often as desired. No one can make fixed rules in this respect.

Neither should it become a routine — a scheduled program which is planned in advance. Otherwise we risk making the love act monotonous. This monotony is often the beginning of dissatisfaction.

The frequency of the conjugal act varies according to age, health and temperament of the couple. I would advise not to unite unless there is a real desire to do so. The partner who has the greater desire should adjust to the one who is less ardent and not the other way around. In any case, excess should be discouraged. Better two times not at all, than one time too much. Some couples like to unite twice a week, others three times. It may also happen that a mutual passion makes them unite every day. But then there may come a time when they wish to abstain for a whole week, or even two. It all depends upon what serves the conjugal peace best.

I cannot close this chapter without speaking about sexual self-control within marriage. Even married people cannot have intercourse at any time they might wish. Sickness, temporary separation while one partner is on a trip, and pregnancy are some of the factors which impose sexual restraint also on a married couple. If one of them is sick and suffering, then he must concentrate all his powers to fight pain and sometimes even the fear of death. In case of temporary separation, each partner lives in chastity in order to keep the conjugal fidelity which he has promised before God.

During pregnancy, abstention from sexual union is recommended during the last four to six weeks before the expected date of birth. Also after the wife has given birth, it is well for the couple to abstain from intimate relations for at least six weeks, when the wife's organs have returned to their normal state.

As you can see, sexual self-control is necessary if a marriage is to be successful. This self-control is not easy to learn and therefore one must begin before marriage. The one who has not learned how to master his passions before marriage will have difficulty mastering them after marriage. Therefore the happiness of his marriage is at stake.

The one who neglects to learn sexual self-control is heading blindly for failure. Good will and human strength alone are not sufficient to learn this self-discipline.

From all that I have said thus far, you may have the impression that all that counts for a successful sexual union is human wisdom and intelligence or simply following good advice in order to reach the goal. If you try this, you will soon experience defeat. Human power alone is not enough for a successful marriage. We would be lost if God himself were not willing to give us his power in order to put this counsel into practice. In order to be able to understand each other and to love each other intimately in the way I have described, it is necessary for each one of us to have a personal relationship with God.

Many couples, when they experience a crisis, forget completely the help and the power of prayer. I know couples who pray together every evening except when they want to unite sexually. They have the impression that the sex act and prayer do not fit together. This means they have separated their sexual life from their spiritual life. They consider the sexual union in marriage often as something dirty or even sinful and have a bad conscience about it. This is a great mistake. It is entirely unbiblical. God is the Lord of all realms of life, and this means also the sexual realm.

God wants to be close to us in whatever we experience and this is true also about the act of love.

FOR FURTHER READING

Bird, Joseph W. and Lois. *The Freedom of Sexual Love.* New York: Doubleday and Company, 1967.

Bovet, Theodor. *A Handbook to Marriage.* New York: Doubleday and Company, 1958.

Deutsch, Ronald M. *The Key to Feminine Response in Marriage.* New York: Ballantine Books, 1968.

Ludlow, Joyce R. *About Your Marriage.* London: Longmans.

Mace, David R. *Whom God Hath Joined.* Philadelphia: Westminister, 1953; London: Epworth, 1953.

Trobisch, Walter. *I Loved a Girl.* New York: Harper and Row, 1965; London: Lutterworth, 1963.

Trobisch, Walter. *Love Is a Feeling to Be Learned.* Downers Grove, Ill.: Inter-Varsity Press, 1969; Baden-Baden: Editions Trobisch, 1969.

Trobisch, Walter. *My Parents Are Impossible.* Downers Grove, Ill.: Inter-Varsity Press, 1970; Baden-Baden: Editions Trobisch, 1970.

Trobisch, Walter. *My Wife Made Me a Polygamist.* Downers Grove, Ill.: Inter-Varsity Press, 1971; Baden-Baden: Editions Trobisch, 1971.

Trobisch, Walter. *Please Help Me! Please Love Me! A Christian View of Contraception.* Downers Grove, Ill.: Inter-Varsity Press, 1970; Baden-Baden: Editions Trobisch, 1970.